Pebble® Plus
Bilingüe/ Bilingual

Cómo hacer un
tornado en una botella
How to Build a
Tornado in a Bottle

A divertirse con la ciencia

Hands-On Science Fun

por/by Lori Shores

Editora consultora/Consulting Editor: Gail Saunders-Smith, PhD

Consultor/Consultant: Ronald Browne, PhD
Departamento de Educación Elemental y de Primera Infancia/
Department of Elementary & Early Childhood Education
Universidad Estatal de Minnesota, Mankato/Minnesota State University, Mankato

CAPSTONE PRESS
a capstone imprint

Pebble Plus is published by Capstone Press,
151 Good Counsel Drive, P.O. Box 669, Mankato, Minnesota 56002.
www.capstonepub.com

Books published by Capstone Press are manufactured with paper
containing at least 10 percent post-consumer waste.

Library of Congress Cataloging-in-Publication Data
Shores, Lori.
 [How to build a tornado in a bottle. Spanish & English]
 Cómo hacer un tornado en una botella = How to build a tornado in a bottle / por Lori Shores.
   p. cm.—(Pebble plus bilingüe. A divertirse con la ciencia = Pebble plus bilingual. Hands-on science fun)
 Summary: "Simple text and full-color photos instruct readers how to build a tornado in a bottle and explain the science
behind the activity—in both English and Spanish"—Provided by publisher.
 Includes index.
 ISBN 978-1-4296-6107-2 (library binding)
 1. Tornadoes—Experiments—Juvenile literature. I. Title. II. Title: How to build a tornado in bottle. III. Series.
QC955.2.S5418 2011
551.55'3078—dc22   2010042263

Editorial Credits
Jenny Marks, editor; Strictly Spanish, translation services; Juliette Peters, designer; Danielle Ceminsky, bilingual book
    designer; Sarah Schuette; photo shoot direction; Marcy Morin, scheduler; Laura Manthe, production specialist

Photo Credits
All photos by Capstone Studio: Karon Dubke except: Dreamstime: Chris White, 17; Shutterstock: Jhaz Photography,
    cover, back cover (background), 1, 2–3, 22, 23, 24, Rafai Fabrykiewicz, 4–5

Safety Note/Nota de seguridad

Please ask an adult for help in building your tornado in a bottle./
Pídele a un adulto que te ayude a crear tu tornado en una botella.

Note to Parents and Teachers

The A divertirse con la ciencia/Hands-On Science Fun set supports national science standards
related to physical science. This book describes and illustrates building a tornado in a bottle
in both English and Spanish. The images support early readers in understanding the text. The
repetition of words and phrases helps early readers learn new words. This book also introduces
early readers to subject-specific vocabulary words, which are defined in the Glossary section.
Early readers may need assistance to read some words and to use the Table of Contents,
Glossary, Internet Sites, and Index sections of the book.

Printed in the United States of America in North Mankato, Minnesota.
092010   005933CGS11

Table of Contents

Tabla de contenidos

Getting Started

The rain pours and the wind roars.
Tornadoes can be scary.
But there's nothing scary
about a tornado in a bottle.

Para empezar

La lluvia cae y el viento ruge.
Los tornados pueden ser
aterradores. Pero un tornado
en una botella no asusta a nadie.

Here's what you need/ Necesitarás:

2 clear 2-liter plastic bottles, clean/2 botellas transparentes de plástico de 2 litros, limpias

duct tape/cinta adhesiva para ductos

3 cups (¾ liter) of water/ 3 tazas (¾ de litro) de agua

blue food coloring/colorante azul para alimentos

Making a Tornado in a Bottle

First, remove the labels from two 2-liter bottles. Then mix a few drops of food coloring into 3 cups (¾ liter) of water. Pour the colored water into one of the bottles.

Cómo hacer un tornado en una botella

Primero, quítales las etiquetas a las dos botellas de 2 litros. Luego mezcla unas cuantas gotas de colorante para alimentos en 3 tazas (¾ de litro) de agua. Vierte el agua de color en una de las botellas.

Place the empty bottle upside-down
on top of the first bottle. Line up
the openings.

Coloca la botella vacía boca abajo
sobre la primera botella.
Alinea los picos de las botellas.

Use duct tape to cover the necks of
the bottles. Wrap the tape tightly
so the bottles won't come apart.

Cubre los cuellos de las botellas
con cinta adhesiva para ductos.
Aprieta muy bien la cinta para que
las botellas no puedan separarse.

Turn the bottles over so the water
is on top. Watch as the water
moves slowly to the bottom.

Da vuelta las botellas para que
el agua quede arriba. Observa
mientras el agua pasa lentamente
a la botella de abajo.

Turn the bottles over again.

Quickly swirl the bottles
in a circle a few times.
Watch as a tornado appears!

Da vuelta las botellas de nuevo.

Agita las botellas rápidamente
en un círculo varias veces.
¡Mira cómo aparece un tornado!

How Does It Work?

Real tornadoes happen when hot air pushes up. Wind whips around a center point, pulling cold air down.

¿Cómo funciona?

Los tornados reales ocurren cuando el aire caliente se eleva. El aire azota un punto central, empujando aire frío hacia abajo.

wind/
viento

cold air/
aire frío

hot air/
aire caliente

The tornado in the bottle works in a similar way. When the bottles are turned over, the air pushes up.

El tornado en la botella funciona de manera similar. Al dar vuelta las botellas, el aire se eleva.

air/
aire

Swirling the bottles around makes the
water spin around the center hole.
Like wind, the movement
pulls the water down.

Al agitar las botellas en círculos,
el agua gira alrededor de un agujero
central. Al igual que el viento,
el movimiento empuja el agua
hacia abajo.

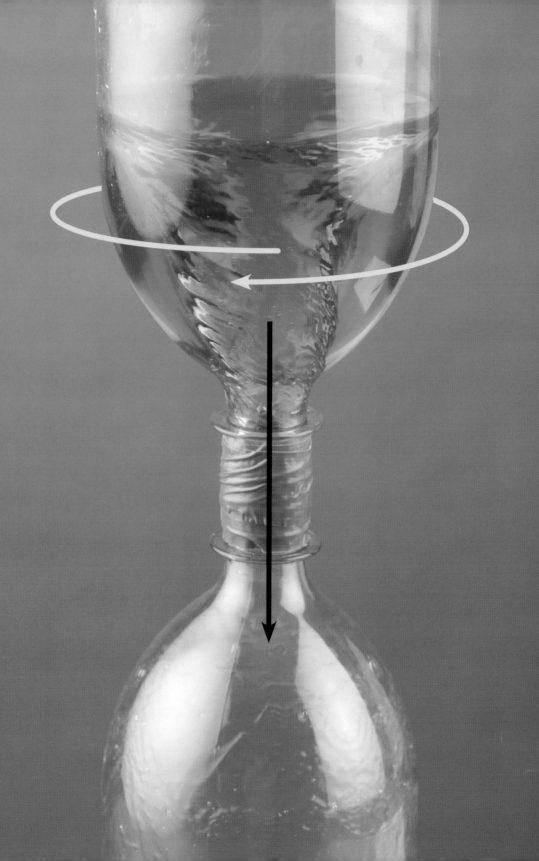

Glossary

roar—to make a loud, deep noise

similar—alike

swirl—to quickly move around in circles

whip—to quickly move with great force

Internet Sites

FactHound offers a safe, fun way to find
Internet sites related to this book. All of the sites
on FactHound have been researched by our staff.

Here's all you do:

Visit www.facthound.com

Type in this code: 9781429661072

Super-cool stuff!

Check out projects, games and lots more at
www.capstonekids.com

Glosario

agitar—mover rápidamente en círculos

azotar—moverse rápidamente con gran fuerza

rugir—hacer un sonido fuerte y grave

similar—parecido

Sitios de Internet

FactHound brinda una forma segura y divertida de encontrar sitios de Internet relacionados con este libro. Todos los sitios en FactHound han sido investigados por nuestro personal.

Esto es todo lo que tienes que hacer:

Visita *www.facthound.com*

Ingresa este código: 9781429661072

¡Algo súper divertido! Hay proyectos, juegos y mucho más en www.capstonekids.com

Index

Índice